BREAKFAST
WITH MARTHA

poems by

Philip Michael Goodman

Published by
Geo. R. Reeve Ltd.
9-11 Town Green, Wymondham,
Norfolk NR18 0BD

ISBN 0 900616 70 9

Printed and published by
Geo. R. Reeve Ltd., 9-11 Town Green, Wymondham, Norfolk.

Further copies may be obtained from Xanthus,
Reymerston, near Norwich, NR9 4RA   Telephone: 01362 850862

CONTENTS

Meeting House 1

Spatter 2

Nightingales at Fenouillet 2

The Comfort of Norfolk 3

Sand-devils at Holkham 4

The Reporter 5

Dusk in the Park 6

Springtime in Cley 7

Opening of the Great Court at the British Museum 8

Breakfast with Martha 9

Sorrow in Winchcombe 10

No Offence Taken 11

Whittington Hospital 12

Bird in House 13

On the Way to Bedford 14

In the Campo of the Ghetto, Venice 15

Bream 16

The Man who Shot the Hare 17

September 18

The Day After Remembrance Day 19

Golf Ball 20

Old Gun Emplacement, Cephalonia 21

At Ickworth 22

Lilac 23

Refugees in a Coach Station 24

Spider on Rayon 25

The Garage Man's Box 26

Summer Afternoon 27

Coup de Soleil in Corsica 27

La Galère 28

Cafe Pigeon 29

On the Cliffs 30

Three Men on a Step 31

Wedding in the Rain 31

Earth Walls 32

The Hereford Road 33

In the Pyrenees 34

Alan and Ronaldo 35

Substance 36

Gargoyle on a 19th Century Cathedral 37

Ajaccio: The Childhood of Napoleon 38

Quaker's Yard 39

Feather Fetishist 39

The Old Field Marshal 40

The Sergeant-Major 41

White Bird 42

Cats 43

Holy Mountain 43

Midnight in County Sligo 44

Millennium 45

Meeting House

The track that seems to lead to no-where
In fact leads true –
To a square building of dimpled brick,
With doves in the roof, watching us;
The inside, a white cube, perfectly simple,
Held up by columns carved in wood,
With a balcony on which some carpenter,
Suddenly playful, has laid twists of ornament.
Our voices ring like bells in that space,
Anglican minds grope for reference,
But none – just four walls faced by plank benches,
A boskiness outside fingering old sash-windows,
The Norfolk light flooding in with such clear authority.

Spatter

The wall we have just painted
With Farrow and Ball terracotta
Is splodged with droppings, overnight,
Messy as a toddler's tantrum.
You blame the blackbirds
Nesting in the gutters, but something
About the mocking, wilful spatter
Says otherwise, and, of course,
It is the rascally starlings;
Diagnosis confirmed
As the clean-smelling morning
Fills with their merriment.

Nightingales at Fenouillet

They come out of the thickets by the gorge
These silken midnights in May
And toss melody at each other
With an abandon they wouldn't dare in the light,
Piccolos trembling above the torrent's bass rush,
Clockwork set precise
By twin fireflies in the west –
A hanging satellite and,
Moving slowly between high peaks,
The night flight to Barcelona,
On time.

The Comfort of Norfolk

Only the unrequited linger, find comfort
In the single dull street, its rhythm of mundane bustle.
Drivers hurry through, nothing to detain them,
A plain, unexceptional town peopled by the old,
Who hang over fish and chips and weak tea in cafes
And watch boys kick dead leaves round the square.
Shoppers peer near-sighted at window-cards
For kittens, worn-out Fiestas, careful lodgers.
Corner pubs, hulking and empty, full of 19th century
Self-importance, elbow the pensioners.

But the seekers partake in the slow disappointment
Of broken awnings against Edwardian sun long set,
Mark how the slipping away of prosperity is almost complete,
Breathe the neighbourhood contagion,
Relish, over and over, the dusty, familiar allure
Of failed expectations.

Sand-devils at Holkham

The sand-devils are loose
Rushing across the beach
In designs subtle and assured
Joyful in the day's wildness
Brawling around our legs
Racing on
To embrace distant devil armies

Shivering pine trees
Bend to the spectacle
In doleful Mexican waves
The grey-brown devils the event
All else anecdote –
Sprinting on
To the sea's fatal winning post

The Reporter

On that gritty provincial newspaper where
"Nice story" was the height of praise,
Only he kept books of poems on his desk.
I can see his Flying Officer Kite moustache
Nosing among the titles, the always-in-a-hurry
Charcoal suit tapering to suede brogues.

A withered arm, or was it a war wound (I never knew),
Made his movements angular and sudden,
Like the flutterings of a damaged umbrella.
The leathery Erroll Flynn face of a piece
With the acerbic charm; a lothario, of course,
And a quiet and serious user of alcohol.

This difficult, enigmatic man wrote fine prose.
When the first edition arrived, there was silence
As people read him, and you felt the dawning
Tough, professional admiration, and resentment;
So much craft, swift simplicity,
Cunning sprinklings, exemplary metaphors.

Nothing was ever said; he was too private and scary.
Did we ever consider
He was offering us his dreams?
Sometimes think of him when I turn a line that chimes:
What would Ted have made of that?
He never told me then: I doubt he would now.

Dusk in the Park

A single light burns
In a flat above Bayswater Road,
Anonymous and steady;
The figures move away from it
Across the park,
Hurrying, straight-legged, to beat the dusk,
Surf of brown leaves underfoot,
Sallow sky darkening by the minute,
The souk of Knightsbridge ahead,
Silhouettes winking gold,
Windows full of leather and silk –
Its commerce
Holding back the night.

Springtime in Cley

Yellow poppies, thin as tissue,
Press out of the stones
Behind a shingle bank –
Yet crave a special palette:

Their gold tossed against
The tide's strange whiteness.
This synchrony denied,
They beat at that confining wall,

Discover its obduracy,
Their own brevity,
Grow frantic
Under the huge sky.

Opening of the Great Court
at the British Museum

London skies tumbling down from Hampstead
Caught panchromatic
In the honeycomb prisms of the roof
And projected
To search blues and golds
Only Ruskin and the Victorians
Saw in this compelling freshness

Strike carved limestone
And caress the Lion of Cnidus
Who turns his head away
Surprised by the vivid Hellenic light

And flood on
To colour the air itself
Exultant with our oxygen of looking

Breakfast with Martha

Uneasy silence – and so early –
As she munches
Seeds, raisins, chopped apple, nuts,
Ben with his marmalade toast
And Scots oats.
She doesn't criticise,
Just this meditative shrinking.
Ben has no appetite for nuts and seeds,
But he finds one when Martha leaves,
And sits mourning
Over the bowl of thin, avine morsels
As if this communion
Can re-assemble those mornings.
Three-hundred breakfasts, then
Porridge, bread, pourings of marmalade
Return, and Ben feasts,
Almost himself again.

Sorrow in Winchcombe

Sudeley Hill shining with ice.
Car slewing on the tarmac.
Smother the revs.
Don't touch the brakes.
Let the old competence
Drop down to the town.

Taken by surprise
By the barmaid's smile
That pierces
Sharper than indifference.
Register like a tourist
The clean limestone of the fireplace
In the snug; turn an ear
To laughter from the bar.

Across the table, a dealing man,
Professionally companionable and rosy;
Has the steak, between mouthfuls
Tells tales of thievery and dishonour,
Holds me listening.
Light flickers on old beams, rows of bottles,
He, benign in his Tudor halo, looks me in the eye,
Unsuspecting.

No Offence Taken

They savour her name on claret breath
As they stand about the mahogany library,
Vistas of beech trees and rhododendrons.
"Not appropriate" – and they clip the word
Into sharp segments. "We'll call her Elizabeth,
Which shortens conveniently to Betsy."

And when they tell Isabella Gallagher, their brogue
Becomes as thick and friendly as the gardener's,

While she, being of gentle, appreciative nature,
Takes no offence at all, and counts her blessings –
Nicely housed in a lodge by the armourial gates,
Hanging out a white wash in the moist, contrary air.

Whittington Hospital

Millions of gothic bricks
Of grey-green urban yellow
Teeter over Archway Road,
Affirming the ambivalence of the place,
Half French chateau, half seaside hotel.
A young woman on her knees
Pressing your chest:
"Breathe, Oliver, Breathe";
Your Windsor-blue eyes
Full of weakness and candour;
I put my ear close –
Urgent, soft, your words are lost;
Beyond the window, lethal tarmac,
Container lorries thunder north.

Bird in House

In all the free-flying dawns,
No presentiment of this confinement –
A hall-of-mirrors against which
The compromised wings beat,

And pandemonium
Among the unfamiliar walls and objects,
Panic droppings across sills,
Fluff of bruised feathers on the floor.

A hand encloses the bird,
And, strangely yielding,
It waits, tiny gaze artless as if
Rediscovering some rudimentary shell,

Before springing into blue air,
Soaring away in a clatter.

On the way to Bedford

Drawing pints with a gravity and elegance
Out of place in this yellowing wayside pub,
A well-kept man, handsome, sardonic,
Hair layered to softly cut suit, white shirt open,
Glance level and supercilious,
Manicured hands counting the small change,
Part Irish chieftain, part French marquis.
The patron's languid menace doesn't go unnoticed –
The drinkers eye themselves
In the mirror of his singularity
And mend their manners,
In a sly and Fenland way.

In the Campo of the Ghetto, Venice

A shaven-headed boy tries to
Kick the parading pigeons, fails;
A tiny man crouched on a seat
Repeats a tuneless song;
Aimlessly, eccentricly,
They people the stone geometry.

Then a sadness curls down
From the big shadowed windows
Of hidden synagogues,
Creeps beneath door-sills and
Hangs further layers of grey
On pitted brick and stone.

A shutter closes, as if
To exclude a familiar miasma;
The sadness lies, chokingly,
In the middle air.

On the bridge to the campo,
A blond, beribboned boatman
Calls "Gondola, gondola..."
His stare is sharp,
Unamiable, *non é simpatico.*

As if disturbed, the sadness
Retreats to upper storeys,
Where it caresses dust lying
On baroque gilt and mahogany

In old sacred rooms;
Abandoned embroideries with
Earth colours of black and ochre
Are brushed by it;
Drinking cups of worn silver
Fill drop by drop;
It rests, footdeep, on the
Dark, empty stairways.

Achingly, the process happens,
While, outside, the campo's blank face
Assumes a waiting look.

Bream

Tipped from grabbing net
To the strangeness of grass
At his captors' mercy
Gills sucking at unresponsive air
Knight's carapace of armoured silver
Inviting the prising knife
Desperate eye fixed open
Horribly deceived
Drowning
In the snare of the morning
A shadow looming
Bending to disgorge hook from tissue
And I walking on
Up the sunny path

The Man who Shot the Hare

Landrover parked cheekily across the forest track,
A tarpaulin, which he pulls aside
And with a friendly smile reveals rows
Of pheasants hung clean as in a larder.
And on the floor, a hare, doggy legs
Splayed drowsily in death, blood at mouth,
Troubling eyes half-shut, unexpected trophy
For this man in search of birds.

A beetle creeps over the York-stone path;
He changes step to crush it.
Inside the house, all as usual,
Daughter bent over homework,
Wife in kitchen, "Good day, sweetie?"
He sinks corduroyed behind on pink moquette
And clicks for the six o'clock news. Instant,
Just like the trigger's smart response,
The hare's abrupt, arrested flight
And shuddering fall to stubble.
He opens a can of light ale and,
With his big man's careful movements, drinks.

September

Swallows and martins
On strands of wire
All lined up
Like music on a sheet
Opening and shutting wings
Cascading away
With African cries
To return, rearrange
Squinny at the south
Ancestral images
Of Saxon church tower
And moist landscape
Womb of flying insects
Dissolving,
Albedos of desert dust
And jungle valleys
Flicker before magic-lantern eyes

The Day after Remembrance Day

He comes limping along Elizabeth Street,
Up from the millionaires' end,
And Vivien Leigh's mansion,
An old soldier, poppy, beret, stick,
Row of medals hanging from rainbow ribbon,
Passing the posh shops – the Chatsworth emporium,
French patisserie, the shop selling shirts
Of plain, weighty cotton, cigar shop,
Picture framer's, the shadowy antique places
Glinting with ormulu and mahogany,
Daring you to enter. To the street's dubious end,
The small assemblage of indispensables –
Grubby sandwich bars, budget winery,
Kebab house, fish and chip shop,
All serving the coach-station, which he enters,
Tip-tapping his way to a seat.

Opposite sits an African girl, glowing like summer
chocolate,
Well wrapped against the London chill,
Ritual marks on face, hair a myriad tiny plaits
With orange beads at tips,
Looking about her with curiosity, quietly considering
The puzzle of this crowded ante-room to the bus
And its journey to the ordained, alien town.
She gazes at the old man. Unexpectedly, he reaches up
And pulls at his medals; they come away
On a single strip of dark linen. And he pockets them.
The African girl looks and goggles,
Her lovely prognathus jaw open,
Sensing the real strangeness of this grey land.

19

Golf Ball

Purchased in the pro's shop
On a fine morning of high hope
Placed on a yellow tee and struck
With cunning, well-considered force
Rising in an arc so pure and sweet
That the players hold their breath
Until a puff of air lofts it
Over a hedge and into the furrows
Of a ploughed field where it lies
Gleaming and surprised like a new-laid egg

Old Gun-Emplacement, Cephalonia

Monstrous spiders have made an empire
Among the path through the minefield,
Suspending huge lace-curtain webs
In which they squat like birds;

The soldiers' trail almost effaced
By the clawed and shrouded shrubs;
Hot sun hammers the place, no coolness
From turquoise sea, only the spiders

Unsubdued, as they watch the soldiers
Keeping watch on Ithaca;
Spiders and men narrow-eyed as Odysseus,
The sentinels' torsos becoming brown:

Golden days, but stained by menace –
Covert weapons part the prickly bush –
And suddenly, the ancient panic that lives
In the wood gathers itself and descends –

The spiders stiffen, abandon their feasts;
The soldiers make a fearful decampment:
Explosives primed, grey denim pressing
Up the trail, humping ammunition boxes

And clean-smelling machine guns, tearing
At the great webs, the spiders scurrying
To escape down firemen's poles of spun silk;
In the distance, muffled by heat, detonations.

That night, the spiders rebuild, harness
Fresh silk, set their traps again,
Full of certainty, voracious, changeless,
As if Odysseus had never died.

At Ickworth

Barely mid-afternoon, yet twilight,
Premature and uneasy,
Presses into the house.
Chandeliers gleam submarine yellow,
Vapour invades corners
Of staterooms painted Pompei red.
The guardians chafe to go home to tea.
A youth looks out at dripping trees,
Brushes the panes of long windows
With white-cotton gloves.

Lilac

Gaudy, unlucky,
Those gross spirals, phallic sugar-cones
Turn to the sun
With such indecent appetite,
Their lush, ancestral smell
Cloying with over-sweetness,
Yet detaining.

I remember how you, whom misfortune
Sought out so dramatically,
Hated lilac, wouldn't have it near.
How well you understood the dark cycle –
Blowsy beauty turning quickly to decay,
Yet the little heart-shaped leaves
Holding fast, domestic and threatening.

Refugees in a Coach Station

Vivaldi on the speakers,
Two sisters pressed together for comfort,
Murmuring in low, Balkan voices,
Mountain faces sharing,
The same arrangement of feature,
But one more beautiful:
Proud cheekbones and mouth,
Slanted eyes, olive skin blushed
By wind and rain.
At her feet, covered in labels
And the scrawls of border-guards, luggage,
Outlandish in its bulging cheapness,
Spills onto the safe London pavement.
She throws back hair streaked by sun
And, as if remembering,
Lets the fierce, vagrant music
Fall on her like a celebration.

Spider on Rayon

The tiniest of spiders tips from above,
Hesitates at the alien surface,
Throws a loop of silk, shimmies to deep grass,

Inquisitive yet incurious,
Purposeful with unknowable
Spider errands;

And careful to leave his trace,
There among the dull synthetic, like
A dropped scarf – one single, shining thread.

The Garage Man's Box

A ruined castle, huge, mysterious –
So we asked the garage man about it,
And he produced a dusty box
Full of ancient artefacts:

Fragments of clay cup and faded glass,
Balls from culverins and muskets,
Hooks on which bloody meat once swung,
A Stuart button, a boar's tusk;

These he rifled through with
The picky fingers of a savant,
Proud, lustful of his hoard,
Knowledgeable as a don.

Evidence laid before our eyes, the
Conjuror clothed dead earthworks with
Pinnacles, turrets, entry-ports,
Tapestried rooms warmed by logs.

Then, slyly, sensing we wanted more,
Shut the box, said cheerio,
And went back to peering
At the undersides of cars.

Summer Afternoon

Small sounds
Lead us to siesta:

The random housefly
Puzzling at recesses;
A distant aircraft
That comes and goes;

Murmurs of drowsy afternoon,
Quickly subsumed
In the clamour of our love-making.

Coup de Soleil in Corsica

Sprawled indulgently in a shallow curl
Of sand, guarded against the swinging sun
By dark glasses, towel, tube of cream,
Yet hoping to lie just long enough for that glare
To work on her mood, deliver its correction –
The hot and cold rigors that suffuse
Like Diazepam.

Dose measured perfectly, here she comes,
Golden and smiling, lightly touched by fever,
Her calm, persistent nature restored.

La Galère

Rhythmic as sleep
Sea noises
Steal through white shutters
Moonlight lays a pathway on the water
Dark reflects silver
Like the black pearls
We saw in St. Paul de Vence
Glittering insects
Hang in the sibilant air
Exquisitely dainty
Relishing our bodies' torpor

Cafe Pigeon

With his absurd clown's gait,
He parades his space –
A dappled precinct beyond the Roman theatre,
Full of colour and tilting angles,
An old plane tree holding it together,
And, as if adjusted to this eccentricity,
The bird's bobbing head
Not quite in tandem with the busy feet.
The man at the table feeds him crumbs.
Women with little dogs, schoolgirls,
Delivery vans, drifting couples,
The bird skitters among them,
Boldly optimistic, this modest stage
Among the chequered cloths
Scarcely enough to contain
All his presumption.

On the Cliffs

Horizon of cold silver,
Fringe of grey woods freshing into green,
An auditorium comfortably marked out,
With us sprawled tiny within the stage-set,
Part of the plot yet amazed by
The exuberance of performance:

A long growl, not unkind, rising from the surf
As it corrugates shingle;
Scalextric cars move purposefully
For pleasure on the switchback coast road,
And a little steam train's flowing plume
Queries the dead sails of a windmill –

The grace-note to Repton's nobbish park,
Man-made hills and schooled plantations
Vying bumptious with the tumble of eroding cliffs,
Stripped downland and the rolling blues and greens
In the Persian carpet sea,
With a fishing boat hanging in the shallows' slick.

On cue, skylarks, conjured
From coverless meadows,
Pour out domestic anthems, breathless.
I look in your unsceptical eyes and see
The whole glittering celebration
Photographed sweetly.

Three Men on a Step

Three men on a step in the City of London:
Washed, rosy, convivial,
Fags in mouth, a bottle or two, their clothes
Decent but clearly someone else's.
Workers in suits – properly bought – pass by,
Blinking from their fluorescent screens,
Examine the group with a tart
"It's OK for some," unable to imagine such freedom.
The three look back, part of the scenery,
Enjoying themselves.

Wedding in the Rain

We huddle outside the grocer's,
Lights ablaze against the downpour,
Rain Perpendicular, like the church.
A jostle of dark umbrellas,
Apricot silk glistening with wet.
But mindful of the record,
Bride and groom scorn shelter,
Steadily outstare the clicking wall of cameras.
A coachman in drooping tophat
Wipes the leather seats of their equippage,
And they depart at a fast trot –
Beneath our moist, approving gaze,
Photographing the moment for ourselves.

Earth Walls

Through the years of dull labour and meagre return,
He never messed with the fairy-castle,
Never took tractor or spade to its earth walls,
Kept his distance, watchful of the ancient taboo,
And pondered its function and geometry,
How hornbeam and thorn threw a curtain wall around,
And twilight peopled it with shadows,
As if the tenants had only gone on an errand.
He bothers when the visitors come,
Goes to the door, neglect everywhere, an old man
Among broken sheds, empty yards –
And the earth walls, crinkled, waiting, sorcery
And disappointment in their folds and ditches.
Carefully he directs the seekers,
Round the head of the field, avoiding the barbed wire.

The Hereford Road

The road that leads out of Wales
Is the best, some people said.
I take the Hereford road,
Through Crucorney and Pontrilas,
The muffling mist coming down
From whaleback hills,
Grey, squat houses, wet slate,
Glistening and despairing;
Gradually, the moping landscape giving way
To long orchards, black and white houses
That sit cosy, cattle against fences,
Church bells sounding across red earth.

Not altogether unkind, Wales,
But nothing ever really spelt out,
The bamboozle of all that beery chat;
Looking you in the eye,
Trying to spot their own melancholy;
Quite unlike the level Hereford gaze,
Peaceful, solidly-bottomed.

One day, when I took the Hereford road for good,
Along with me came this Celtic fret
That makes me peer in strangers' eyes –
Seeking that rain-smudged sadness.

In the Pyrenees

Wide-open town,
Not quite Spain, nor yet France;
Everyone gathered at the emporium
For dégustation libre:
Eight different sherries,
Four marsalas and various muscats.
All sweet and cloying,
With little red taps and paper cups
To catch the liquid in. Thoughtful
Trays of olives stand by a notice
Asking you not to get the kids drunk;
Floor slimy with droppings from
Greedy swallowings, and somewhere beyond,
An overflowing lavatory.
Flushed faces press at the windows, wanting more,
As we exit across a pave tesselated
With tossing waves, on which, despite ourselves,
We stagger tipsily.

Alan and Ronaldo

Sashaying between Pembroke tables
And ormulu clocks
So pleased with themselves
Alan and Ronaldo
In carefully matched
Chinos and cashmere sweaters
Cheque-books at hip
Boyishly acquisitive and knowing
Scattering patronage
And their peculiar charm
Oblivious to the softlings –
Snubbed so many times –
Who are about to snatch
That rose-madder Turkish rug
From beneath the tasselled loafers
Bought in Tuscany
On a golden afternoon

Substance

He would pause by a gateway or stile
Take out a handkerchief
Spit on it and gently remove
The small-boy messiness from my cheek
I recoiling a little at this imposition
The spit's gamy edge, sharp familial flavour
There were other tendernesses
But none more unmeditated –
My chin cupped in that large hand
He, keen-eyed,
Carefully cleaning me
With his substance

Gargoyle on a
19th Century Cathedral

The Duke of Norfolk put him here in 1884,
Impious and mocking, leering down
At bonnets, thrusting crinolines, not fish nor fowl,
A freak conjured out of pitchy forests, forbidden lakes.
The devout, decked in their best, shrink when they catch
The outcast's gothic eye upon them,
And the gargoyle, miffed, stares harder.

Century passes. No more nostrils pinched by incense,
A vocabulary of feeling extinguished,
And no talk of "souls", the masses diverted
By soap opera, multi-screens and Tesco;
This cheerful secularity is to the gargoyle's taste –
A much better piece of casting –
And his alarming granite look has softened to a smile.

Ajaccio: the Childhood of Napoleon

A child playing with a toy
On a shaded landing
In a house tightly shut
Against the heat
And the sounds of the harbour,
Scratches a stucco wall
Of grey, provincial chic;
A young woman, clicking
Up the stone staircase
In ribboned shoes,
Seizes him hard and cries
"Petit scélérat..."
The boy's acquiline lips
Open in shock...
Quickly gentle, she
Breathes in his ear
Small noises,
Propitiatory;
At last he turns to her,
Eyes full of candour,
Her blank, fond smile,
Mother and son,
Perfect complicity.

Quaker's Yard

Having considered the pub and its smells
Of rancid beer and smouldering coals,
And the bluff effusiveness of the locals,
That counts here as inscrutability,
Go outside, where there is frost on the black tarmac,
Gleaming orange under sodium light,
Leading upwards only to the pillaged mountainside;
The tinkle of water somewhere
And monochrome houses dropping away
In a staircase of slate roofs;
And beneath your feet, unseeable, deserted galleries
Groined with the picks and shovels of men
Whose white youth was emptied in this darkness,
At fifty coughed up grey phlegm in the street and gasped
A boyo joke at the deadliness of it all.

Feather Fetishist

I asked why
She teased feathers
From plump, blameless pillows,
Her safebreaker's fingers
Kneading the hackle
Out of their dark depositories,
And she replied –
Because it's so satisfying, of course

The Old Field Marshal

Go on, shake the field marshal's hand,
Make the most of this rare encounter –
The hero himself in mufti:
Double-breasted suit fits the compact figure
Snug as battledress,
A hot iron's secret polish at elbow and knee,
Bony fingers that signed treaties and surrenders,
Yet impatient with pockets,
Grasp our own cordially;
The big leaflike ears on the neat head,
Once exactly tuned to the shift in a barrage,
Listening to our nothings;
Monarchs envied the battlefield predator
The completeness of his renown,
But note the cost of this pre-eminence –
The hangman frisson that encloses him,
The will-power in the mild clerical gaze,
The barrier between him and us.
Go on, shake his hand,
Match his jauntiness.

The Sergeant-major

He was once a lion king,
Holding subjects in sway
With a drillstick and his stare,
And what personality couldn't order,
He crushed with the Manual of Military Law.
Pedantic, always right, brassoed and blancoed,
His ironing-board figure
Swung across parade grounds,
Lesser beings clearing a path.

Now mere civilian,
He preens in a different setting,
Outside a large hotel in Piccadilly,
A fairground huckster, Ruritanian
In top hat, frock coat and gold braid,
Who opens the doors of limousines,
Bids lordlings and city types welcome,
Proclaims the importance of the place,
Monitoring gaze impartial
To lolling, hung-over pop stars,
Long hair, stubble, scruffy footwear;
Good-humoured and obsequious,
Yet not undignified,
A £10 note will buy his entire co-operation.

The make-over seems hard,
But at nights the sergeant-major sleeps like a baby.

White Bird

Driving on a country road
On a bitter night, late,
I saw in my lights
A big white bird
Sitting astride the tarmac,
Not disquieted,
As if misfortune
Were part of some norm.
I took the bird home,
Wildness quiescent. But
Next day the bird was dead,
Eyes closed, wings folded,
All shut down, neatly.

I see the bird in life,
Threading across
Salt estuaries above
Clanging markers,
Volant on those
Dependable wings;
To clog them now with earth
Seemed unfitting.
I found a large tree and lodged
This nomad where the trunk forked,
Left him there,
An Iroquois,
Handsome, comfortable.

Cats

When you lie gasping
On some hospital bed
Sustained by myriad
Wires and systems,
They will come –
Lithe, Egyptian-faced –
And trash your tubes
And cover you with black hairs.

Holy Mountain

Going strongly for the top
This barefoot man
Bloodied by bristling
Quartz and granite
The long Celtic face
A blank mask
Alone, in silence
He crosses the cruel scree
Back set against distant
Islets and hills dancing in sunlight
Strangely sure-footed
Out of sight into cloudlands
Where the summit hides –
Its stony eye measuring
Such impunity

Midnight in County Sligo

The eiderdown against summer's
Fickleness, pushed away.
Suddenly awake... This brightness
Through old sash-windows,
The mountain silhouetted by light;
Clear as day, the megalith
Brooding in its field;
Breeze stirring the fuchsia;
An aviary of poles, for the utilities,
Pinning the white houses to the hillside.
A car, over-revved, hesitates
At the broken-backed bridge, goes on.
Silence rushes back – and in that moment
The mountain glow extinguishes
And the room dark at last.

Millennium

In the time it took Carter's boy
To grow from wheedling infant to ominous youth,
Everything changes in an alteration
So determined and complete that accustomed things
Are relinquished without fuss.
Indeed protest seems indecent
Against the replacements
Put in place by the late 20th century...

The wooden seat on which old men sunned themselves
Has gone before the old men. The drab, sawdust pubs,
Havens of sorts for fieldworkers, close one by one.
The village shop that for a hundred years sold
Elixirs for coughs, lamp oil and humbugs,
Doesn't open one day, leaping bell haltered,
Mistress carried to a home for the aged.
Church Farm, where an ancient widow and families
Of owls blinked out at forgotten meadows
Grazed by old horses, becomes a golf club,
Oak-canopied barns, weekenders' retreats.
The last incumbent of the Angevin church shuts himself
In his rectory, nervous breakdown diagnosed.
The Historic Churches' Trust rebuilds the clerestory.
A cassocked lady ministers at the altar, serenely
Dividing her time between a dozen churches
Whose parishioners don't talk to strangers.
Monstrous machines creep over phosphorous praries,
Field margins as old as Danegeld grubbed up.

At dusk, the row of bungalows – once outrageous –
Draw blinds, the inhabitants settle to television.
Unstoppable owls begin to call. Rain falls quietly
Through a dense mediaeval blackness.
Familiar habits, and their nuances, fall away.
A thousand years of history hangs unrecorded.
The stubborn, rampartless fields and cottages
Hide, quiescent in the darkness, and
Millennium bells rise and fall.